OUT OF THIS WORLD
&
THE SEARCH

OUT *of this* WORLD
&
THE SEARCH

NEVILLE
GODDARD

THE NEVILLE COLLECTION

CONTENTS

I.

Thinking Fourth Dimensionally

And now I have told you before it come to pass, that,
when it is come to pass, ye might believe.

—John 14:29

MANY persons, myself included, have observed events before they occurred; that is, before they occurred in this world of three dimensions. Since man can observe an event before it occurs in the three dimensions of space, life on earth must proceed according to plan, and this plan must exist elsewhere in another dimension and be slowly moving through our space.

If the occurring events were not in this world when they were observed, then, to be perfectly logical, they must have been out of this world. And whatever is *there* to be seen before it occurs *here* must be "Predetermined" from the point of view of man awake in a three-dimensional world. Thus the question arises: "Are we able to alter our future?"

My object in writing these pages is to indicate possibilities inherent in man, to show that man can alter his future; but, thus altered, it forms again a deterministic sequence starting from the point of interference—a future that will be consistent with the alteration. The most remarkable feature of man's future is its flexibility. It is determined by his attitudes rather than by his acts. The cornerstone on which all things are based is man's concept of himself. He acts as he does and has the experiences that he does, because his concept of himself is what it is, and for no other reason. Had he a different concept of self, he would act differently. A change of concept of self automatically alters his future: and a change in any term of his future series of experiences reciprocally alters his concept of self. Man's assumptions which he regards as insignificant produce effects that are considerable; therefore man should revise his estimate of an assumption, and recognize its creative power.

All changes take place in consciousness. The future, although prepared in every detail in advance, has several outcomes. At every moment of our lives we have before us the choice of which of several futures we will choose.

There are two actual outlooks on the world possessed by everyone—a natural focus and a spiritual focus. The ancient teachers called the one "the carnal mind," the other "the mind of Christ." We may differentiate them as ordinary waking consciousness—governed by our senses, and a controlled imagination—governed by desire. We recognize these two distinct centers of thought in the statement: "The natural man receiveth not the things of the spirit of God for they are foolishness unto him; neither can he know them for they are spiritually discerned" (1 Corinthians 2:14). The natural view confines reality to the moment called *now*. To the natural view, the past and future are purely imaginary. The spiritual view, on the other hand, sees the contents of time. It sees events as distinct and separated as objects in space. The past and future are a present whole to the spiritual view. What is mental and subjective to the natural man is concrete and objective to the spiritual man.

The habit of seeing only that which our senses permit, renders us totally blind to what we otherwise could see. To cultivate the faculty of seeing the invisible, we should often deliberately disentangle our minds from the evidence of the senses and focus our attention on an invisible state, mentally feeling it and sensing it until it has all the distinctness of reality.

Earnest, concentrated thought focused in a particular direction shuts out other sensations and causes them to disappear. We have but to concentrate on the state desired in order to see it. The habit of withdrawing attention from the region of sensation and concentrating it on the invisible develops our spiritual outlook and enables us to penetrate beyond the world of sense and to see that which is invisible. "For the invisible things of him from the creation of the world are clearly seen" (Romans 1:20). This vision is completely independent of the natural faculties. Open it and quicken it! Without it, these instructions are useless, for "the things of the spirit are spiritually discerned."

A little practice will convince us that we can, by controlling our imagination, reshape our future in harmony with our desire. Desire is the mainspring of action. We could not move a single finger unless we had a desire to move it. No matter what we do, we follow the desire which at the moment dominates our minds. When we break a habit, our desire to break it is greater than our desire to continue in the habit.

The desires which impel us to action are those that

hold our attention. A desire is but an awareness of something we lack or need to make our life more enjoyable. Desires always have some personal gain in view, the greater the anticipated gain, the more intense is the desire. There is no absolutely unselfish desire. Where there is nothing to gain there is no desire, and consequently no action.

The spiritual man speaks to the natural man through the language of desire. The key to progress in life and to the fulfillment of dreams lies in ready obedience to its voice. Unhesitating obedience to its voice is an immediate assumption of the wish fulfilled. To desire a state is to have it. As Pascal has said, "You would not have sought me had you not already found me." Man, by assuming the feeling of his wish fulfilled, and then living and acting on this conviction, alters the future in harmony with his assumption.

Assumptions awaken what they affirm. As soon as man assumes the feeling of his wish fulfilled, his four-dimensional self finds ways for the attainment of this end, discovers methods for its realization. I know of no clearer definition of the means by which we realize our desires than to *experience in imagination what we would experience in the flesh were we to achieve our goal.* This experience of the end wills the means. With its larger outlook the four-dimensional self then constructs the means necessary to realize the accepted end.

The undisciplined mind finds it difficult to assume a state which is denied by the senses. Here is a technique that makes it easy to encounter events before they occur, to "call things which are not seen as though they were" (Romans 4:17). People have a habit of slighting the importance of simple things; but this simple formula for changing the future was discovered after years of searching and experimenting. The first step in changing the future is *desire*—that is: define your objective—know definitely what you want. Secondly: construct an event which you believe you would encounter *following* the fulfillment of your desire—an event which implies fulfillment of your desire—something that will have the action of *self* predominant. Thirdly: immobilize the physical body and induce a condition akin to sleep—lie on a bed or relax in a chair and imagine that you are sleepy; then, with eyelids closed and your attention focused on the action you intend to experience—in imagination—mentally feel yourself right into the proposed action—imagining all the while that you are actually performing the action here and now. You must always participate in the imaginary action, not merely stand back and look on, but you must feel that you are actually performing the action so that the imaginary sensation is real to you.

It is important always to remember that the proposed action must be one which *follows* the fulfillment of your desire; and, also, you must feel yourself into the action until it has all the vividness and distinctness of reality. For example: suppose you desired promotion in office. Being congratulated would be an event you would encounter following the fulfillment of your desire. Having selected this action as the one you will experience in imagination, immobilize the physical body, and induce a state akin to sleep—a drowsy state—but one in which you are still able to control the direction of your thoughts—a state in which you are attentive without effort. Now, imagine that a friend is standing before you. Put your imaginary hand into his. First feel it to be solid and real, then carry on an imaginary conversation with him in harmony with the action. Do not visualize yourself at a distance in point of space and at a distance in point of time being congratulated on your good fortune. Instead, make elsewhere *here*, and the future *now*. The future event is a reality *now* in a dimensionally larger world; and, oddly enough, *now* in a dimensionally larger world, is equivalent to *here* in the ordinary three-dimensional space of everyday life. The difference between *feeling* yourself in action, here and now, and visualizing yourself in action, as though you were on a motion-picture screen, is the difference between success and failure. The difference will be appreciated if you will now visualize yourself climbing a ladder. Then with eyelids closed imagine that a ladder is right in front of you and *feel* you are actually climbing it.

Desire, physical immobility bordering on sleep, and imaginary action in which self feelingly predominates, *here and now*, are not only important factors in altering the future, but they are essential conditions in consciously projecting the spiritual self. If, when the physical body is immobilized we become possessed of the idea to do some thing—and imagine that we are doing it *here and now* and keep the imaginary action feelingly going right up until sleep ensues—we are likely to awaken out of the physical body to find ourselves in a dimensionally larger world with a dimensionally larger focus and actually doing what we desired and imagined we were doing in the flesh. But whether we awaken there or not, we are actually performing the action in the fourth-dimensional world, and we will re-enact it in the future, here in the third-dimensional world.

Experience has taught me to restrict the imaginary action, to condense the idea which is to be the object of our meditation into a single act, and to re-enact it over and over again until it has the feeling of reality. Otherwise, the attention will wander off along an associational track, and hosts of associated images will be presented to our attention. In a few seconds they will lead us hundreds of miles away from our objective in point of space, and years away in point of time. If we decide to climb a particular flight of stairs, because that is the likely event to follow the realization of our desire, then we must restrict the action to climbing that particular flight of stairs. Should our attention wander off, we must bring it back to its task of climbing that flight of stairs and keep on doing so until the imaginary action has all the solidity and distinctness of reality. The idea must be maintained in the field of presentation without any sensible effort on our part. We must, with the minimum of effort, permeate the mind with the feeling of the wish fulfilled.

Drowsiness facilitates change because it favors attention without effort, but it must not be pushed to the stage of sleep, in which we shall no longer be able to control the movements of our attention, but rather a moderate degree of drowsiness in which we are still able to direct our thoughts. A most effective way to embody a desire is to assume the feeling of the wish fulfilled and then, in a relaxed and sleepy state, repeat over and over again, like a lullaby, any short phrase which implies fulfillment of our desire, such as "Thank you" as though we addressed a higher power for having done it for us. If, however, we seek a conscious projection into a dimensionally larger world, then we must keep the action going right up until sleep ensues.

Experience in imagination, with all the distinctness of reality, what would be experienced in the flesh were you to achieve your goal; and you shall, in time, meet it in the flesh as you met it in your imagination. Feed the mind with *premises*—that is, assertions *presumed* to be true, because assumptions, though unreal to the senses, if persisted in, until they have the *feeling of reality*, will harden into facts. To an assumption all means which promote its realization are good. It influences the behavior of all by inspiring in all the movements, the actions, and the words which tend towards its fulfillment.

To understand how man molds his future in harmony with his assumption we must know what we mean by a dimensionally larger world, for it is to a dimensionally larger world that we go to alter our future. The observation of an event before it occurs implies that the event is predetermined from the point of view of man in the three-dimensional world. Therefore, to change the conditions here in the three dimensions of space we must first change them in the four dimensions of space.

Man does not know exactly what is meant by a dimensionally larger world, and would no doubt deny the existence of a dimensionally larger self. He is quite familiar with the three dimensions of length, width and height, and he feels that if there were a fourth dimension, it should be just as obvious to him as the dimensions of length, width and height. A dimension is not a line; it is any way in which a thing can be measured that is entirely different from all other ways. That is, to measure a solid fourth-dimensionally, we simply measure it in any direction except that of its length, width and height.

Is there another way of measuring an object other than those of its length, width and height? Time measures my life without employing the three dimensions of length, width and height. There is no such thing as an instantaneous object. Its appearance and disappearance are measurable. It endures for a definite length of time. We can measure its life span without using the dimensions of length, width and height. Time is definitely a fourth way of measuring an object.

The more dimensions an object has, the more substantial and real it becomes. A straight line, which lies entirely in one dimension, acquires shape, mass and substance by the addition of dimensions. What new quality would time, the fourth dimension, give which would make it just as vastly superior to solids as solids are to surfaces and surfaces are to lines? Time is a medium for changes in experience because all changes take time. The new quality is changeability.

Observe that if we bisect a solid, its cross section will be a surface; by bisecting a surface, we obtain a line; and by bisecting a line, we get a point. This means that a point is but a cross section of a line, which is, in turn, but a cross section of a surface, which is, in turn, but a cross section of a solid, which is, in turn, if carried to its logical conclusion, but a cross section of a four-dimensional object.

We cannot avoid the inference that all three-dimensional objects are but cross sections of four-dimensional bodies. Which means: when I meet you, I meet a cross section of the four-dimensional you—the four-dimension *self* that is not seen. To see the four-dimensional *self* I must see every cross section or moment of your life from birth to death and see them all as coexisting. My focus should take in the entire array of sensory impressions which you have experienced on earth plus those you might encounter. I should see them, not in the order in which they were experienced by you, but as a present whole. Because *change* is the characteristic of the fourth dimension, I should see them in a state of flux as a living, animated whole.

If we have all this clearly fixed in our minds, what does it mean to us in this three-dimensional world? It means that, if we can move along time's length, we can see the future and alter it as we so desire. This world, which we think so solidly real, is a shadow out of which and beyond which we may at any time pass. It is an abstraction from a more fundamental and dimensionally larger world—a more fundamental world abstracted from a still more fundamental and dimensionally larger world and so on to infinity. The absolute is unattainable by any means or analysis, no matter how many dimensions we add to the world.

Man can prove the existence of a dimensionally larger world simply by focusing his attention on an invisible state and imagining that he sees and feels it. If he remains concentrated in this state, his present environment will pass away, and he will awaken in a dimensionally larger world where the object of his contemplation will be seen as a concrete objective reality. Intuitively I feel that, were he to abstract his thoughts from this dimensionally larger world and retreat still farther within his mind, he would again bring about an externalization of time. He would discover that every time he retreats into his inner mind and brings about an externalization of time, space becomes dimensionally larger. And he would, therefore, conclude that both time and space are serial, and that the drama of life is but the climbing of a multitudinous dimensional time block.

Scientists will one day explain *why* there is a Serial Universe. But in practice how we use this Serial Universe to change the future is more important. To change the future, we need only concern ourselves with two worlds in the infinite series, the world we know by reason of our bodily organs, and the world we perceive independently of our bodily organs.

2.

ASSUMPTIONS
BECOME FACTS

*M*EN believe in the reality of the external world because they do not know how to focus and condense their powers to penetrate its thin crust. This book has only one purpose—the removing of the veil of the senses—the traveling into another world. To remove the veil of the senses we do not employ great effort; the objective world vanishes by turning our attention away from it.

We have only to concentrate on the state desired in order to mentally see it, but to give it reality so that it will become an objective fact, we must focus attention upon the invisible state until it has the feeling of reality. When, through concentrated attention, our desire appears to possess the distinctness and feeling of reality, we have given it the right to become a visible concrete fact.

If it is difficult to control the direction of your attention while in a state akin to sleep, you may find gazing fixedly into an object very helpful. Do not look at its surface but into and beyond any plain object such as a wall, a carpet, or any other object which possesses depth. Arrange it to return as little reflection as possible. Imagine then that in this depth you are seeing and hearing what you want to see and hear until your attention is exclusively occupied by the imagined state. At the end of your meditation, when you awake from your "controlled waking dream," you feel as though you had returned from a great distance. The visible world which you had shut out returns to consciousness and by its very presence informs you that you have been self-deceived into believing that the object of your contemplation was real. But, if you know that consciousness is the one and only reality, you will remain faithful to your vision, and by this sustained mental attitude confirm your gift of reality, and prove that you have the power to give reality to your desires that they may become visible concrete facts.

Define your ideal and concentrate your attention upon the idea of identifying yourself with your ideal. Assume the feeling of being it, the feeling that would be yours were you already the embodiment of your ideal.

Then live and act upon this conviction. This assumption, though denied by the senses, *if persisted in*, will become fact. You will know when you have succeeded in fixing the desired state in consciousness by simply looking *mentally* at the people you know. In dialogues with yourself you are less inhibited and more sincere than in actual conversations with others, therefore the opportunity for self-analysis arises when you are surprised by your mental conversations with others. If you see them as you formerly saw them, you have not changed your concept of self, for all changes of concepts of self result in a changed relationship to your world.

In your meditation allow others to see you as they would see you were this new concept of self a concrete fact. You always seem to others an embodiment of the ideal you inspire. Therefore, in meditation, when you contemplate others, you must be seen by them mentally as you would be seen by them physically were your concept of self an objective fact; that is, in meditation you imagine that they see you expressing that which you desire to be.

If you assume that you are what you want to be your desire is fulfilled, and, in fulfillment, all longing is neutralized. You cannot continue desiring what you have already realized. Your desire is not something you labor to fulfill, it is recognizing something you already possess. It is assuming the feeling of *being* that which you desire to be. Believing and being are one. The conceiver and his conception are one, therefore that which you conceive yourself to be can never be so far off as even to be near, for nearness implies separation. "If thou canst believe, all things are possible to him that believeth" (Mark 9:23). Being is the substance of things hoped, the evidence of things not yet seen (Hebrews 11:1). If you assume that you are what you want to be, then you will see others as they are related to your assumption

If, however, it is the good of others that you desire, then, in meditation, you must represent them to yourself as already being that which you desire them to be. It is through desire that you rise above your present sphere and the road from longing to fulfillment is shortened as you experience in imagination what you would experience in the flesh were you already the embodiment of the ideal you desire to be.

I have stated that man has at every moment of time the choice before him which of several futures he will encounter; but the question arises; "How is that possible when the experiences of man, awake in the three-dimensional world, are predetermined?" as his observation of an event before it occurs implies. This ability to change the future will be seen if we liken the experiences of life on earth to this printed page. Man experiences events on earth singly and successively in the same way that you are now experiencing the words of this page.

Imagine that every word on this page represents a single sensory impression. To get the context, to understand my meaning, you focus your vision of the first word in the upper left-hand corner and then move your focus across the page from left to right, letting it fall on the words singly and successively. By the time your eyes reach the last word on this page you have extracted my meaning. Suppose, however, on looking at the page, with all the printed words thereon equally present, you decided to rearrange them. You could, by rearranging them, tell an entirely different story; in fact; you could tell many different stories.

A dream is nothing more than uncontrolled four-dimensional thinking, or the rearrangement of both past and future sensory impressions. Man seldom dreams of events in the order in which he experiences them when awake. He usually dreams of two or more events which are separated in time, fused into a single sensory impression; or, in his dream, he so completely rearranges his single waking sensory impressions that he does not recognize them when he encounters them in his waking state.

For example; I dreamed that I delivered a package to the restaurant in my apartment building. The hostess said to me, "You can't leave that there"; whereupon, the elevator operator gave me a few letters and as I thanked him for them, he, in turn, thanked me. At this point, the night elevator operator appeared and waved a greeting to me. The following day, as I left my apartment, I picked up a few letters which had been placed at my door. On my way down I gave the day elevator operator a tip and thanked hem for taking care of my mail; whereupon, he thanked me for the tip. On my return home that day I overheard a doorman say to a delivery man, "You can't leave that there." As I was about to take the elevator up to my apartment, I was attracted by a familiar face in the restaurant, and, as I looked in, the hostess greeted me with a smile. Late that night I escorted my dinner guests to the elevator and as I said good-bye to them, the night operator waved goodnight to me.

By simply rearranging a few of the single sensory impressions I was destined to encounter, and by fusing two or more of them into single sensory impressions, I constructed a dream which differed quite a bit from my waking experience.

When we have learned to control the movements of our attention in the four-dimensional world, we shall be able to consciously create circumstances in the three-dimensional world. We learn this control through the waking dream, where our attention can be maintained without effort, for *attention minus effort* is indispensable to changing the future. We can, in a controlled waking dream, consciously construct an event which we desire to experience in the three-dimensional world.

The sensory impressions we use to construct our waking dream are present realities displaced in time or the four-dimensional world. All that we do in constructing the waking dream is to select from the vast array of sensory impressions those, which, when they are properly arranged, imply that we have realized our desire. With the dream clearly defined we relax in a chair and induce a state of consciousness akin to sleep—a state, which, although bordering on sleep, leaves us in conscious control of the movements of our attention. When we have achieved that state, we experience in imagination what we would experience in reality were this waking dream an objective fact. In applying this technique to change the future it is important always to remember that the only thing which occupies the mind during the waking dream is the waking dream, the predetermined action which implies the fulfillment of our desire. How the waking dream becomes physical fact is not our concern. Our acceptance of the waking dream as physical reality wills the means for its fulfillment.

Let me again lay the foundation of changing the future, which is nothing more than a controlled waking dream.

1. Define your objective–know definitely what you want.

2. Construct an event which you believe you will encounter *following* the fulfillment of your desire—something which will have the action of *self* predominant—an event which implies the fulfillment of your desire.

3. Immobilize the physical body and induce a state of consciousness akin to sleep; then, mentally feel yourself right into the proposed action—imagining all the while that you are actually performing the action *here* and *now* so that you experience in imagination what you would experience in the flesh were you now to realize your goal.

Experience has convinced me that this is the perfect way to achieve my goal. However, my own many failures would convict me were I to imply that I have completely mastered the movements of my attention. I can, however, with the ancient teacher say: "This one thing I do, forgetting those things which are behind, and reaching forth unto those things which are before, I press toward the mark for the prize." (Philippians 3:1–14.)

3.

POWER OF
IMAGINATION

Ye shall know the truth, and the truth shall make you
free.   —JOHN 8:32

*M*EN claim that a true judgment must conform to
the external reality to which it relates. This
means that if I, while imprisoned, suggest to myself that
I am free and succeed in believing that I am free, it is
true that I believe in my freedom; but it does not follow
that I am free for I may be the victim of illusion. But,
because of my own experiences, I have come to believe
in so many strange things that I see little reason to doubt
the truth of things that are beyond my experience.

The ancient teachers warned us not to judge from
appearances because, said they, the truth need not conform to the external reality to which it relates. They

claimed that we bore false witness if we imagined evil against another—that no matter how real our belief appears to be—how truly it conforms to the external reality to which it relates—if it does not make free the one of whom we hold the belief, it is untrue and therefore a false judgment.

We are called upon to deny the evidence of our senses and to imagine as true of our neighbor that which makes him free. "Ye shall know the truth, and the truth shall make you free." To know the truth of our neighbor we must assume that he is already that which he desires to be. Any concept we hold of another that is short of his fulfilled desire will not make him free and therefore cannot be the truth.

Instead of learning my craft in schools where attending courses and seminars is considered a substitute for self-acquired knowledge, my schooling was devoted almost exclusively to the power of imagination. I stayed for hours imagining myself to be other than that which my reason and my senses dictated until the imagined states were vivid as reality—so vivid that passer-by became but a part of my imagination and acted as I would have them. By the power of imagination my fantasy led theirs and dictated to them their behavior and the discourse they held together while I was identified with my imagined state. Man's imagination is the man himself, and the world as imagination sees it is the real world, but it is our duty to imagine all that is lovely and of good report (Philippians 4:8). "For the Lord seeth not as man seeth; for man looketh on the outward appearance, but the Lord looketh on the heart" (1 Samuel 16:7). "As a man thinketh in his heart so is he" (Proverbs 23:7).

In meditation, when the brain grows luminous, I find my imagination endowed with the magnetic power to attract to me whatsoever I desire. Desire is the power imagination uses to fashion life about me as I fashion it within myself. I first desire to see a certain person or scene, and then I look *as though I were seeing* that which I want to see, and the imagined state becomes objectively real. I desire to hear, and then I listen *as though I were hearing*, and the imagined voice speaks that which I dictate as though it had initiated the message. I could give you many examples to prove my arguments, to prove that these imagined states do become physical realities; but I know that my examples will awaken in all who have not met the like or who are not inclined towards my arguments, a most natural incredulity. Nevertheless, experience has convinced me of the truth of the statement, "He calleth those things which be not as though they were" (Romans 4:17). For I have, in intense meditation, called things that were not seen as though they were, and the unseen not only became seen, but eventually became physical realities.

By this method—first desiring and then imagining that we are experiencing that which we desire to experience—we can mold the future in harmony with our desire. But let us follow the advice of the prophet and think only the lovely and the good, for the imagination waits on us as indifferently and as swiftly when our nature is evil as when it is good. From us spring forth good and evil. "I have set before thee this day life and good, and death and evil" (Deuteronomy 30:15).

Desire and imagination are the enchanter's wand of fable and they draw to themselves their own affinities. They break forth best when the mind is in a state akin to sleep. I have written with some care and detail the method I use to enter the dimensionally larger world, but I shall give one more formula for opening the door of the larger world. "In a dream, in a vision of the night, when deep sleep falleth upon men, in slumberings upon the bed; Then he openeth the ears of men, and sealeth their instruction" (Job 33:15–16).

In dream we are usually the servant of our vision rather than its master, but the *internal fantasy* of dream can be turned into an *external reality*. In dream, as in mediation, we slip from this world into a dimensionally larger world, and I know that the forms in dream are not flat two-dimensional images which modern psychologists believe them to be. They are substantial realities of the dimensionally larger world, and I can lay hold of them. I have discovered that, if I surprise myself dreaming, I can lay hold of any inanimate or stationary form of the dream—a chair—a table—a stairway—a tree—and command to awake, while firmly holding on the object of the dream, I am pulled through myself with the distinct feeling of awakening from dream. I awaken in another sphere holding the object of my dream, to find that I am no longer the servant of my vision but its master, for I am fully conscious and in control of the movements of my attention. It is in this fully conscious state, when we are in control of the direction of thought, that we call things that are not seen as though they were. In this state we call things by wishing and assuming the feeling of our wish fulfilled. Unlike the world of three dimensions where there is an interval between our assumption and its fulfillment, in the dimensionally larger world there is an immediate realization of our assumption. The external reality instantly mirrors our assumption. Here there is no need to wait four months till harvest. We look again as though we saw, and lo and behold, the fields are already white to harvest.

In this dimensionally larger world "Ye shall not need to fight, set yourselves, stand ye still and see the salvation of the Lord with you" (2 Chronicles 20:17). And because that greater world is slowly passing through our three-dimensional world, we can by the power of imagination mold our world in harmony with our desire. Look *as though you saw*; listen *as though you heard*; stretch forth your imaginary hand *as though you touched*. . . . And your assumptions will harden into facts.

To those who believe that a true judgment must conform to the external reality to which it relates, this will be foolishness and a stumbling block (1 Corinthians 1:23). But I preach and practice the fixing in consciousness of that which man desires to realize. Experience convinces me that fixed attitudes of mind which do not conform to the external reality to which they relate and are therefore called imaginary—"things which are not"—will, nevertheless, "bring to nought things that are" (1 Corinthians 1:28).

I do not wish to write a book of wonders, but rather to turn man's mind back to the one and only reality that the ancient teachers worshipped as God. All that was said of God was in reality said of man's consciousness so we may say, "that, according as it is written, He that glorieth, let him glory in his own consciousness" (I Corinthians 1:31).

No man needs help to direct him in the application of this law of consciousness. "I am" is the self-definition of the absolute. The root out of which everything grows. "I am the vine" (John 15:1; 15:5).

What is your answer to the eternal question, "Who am I?" Your answer determines the part you play in the world's drama. Your answer—that is, your concept of self—need not conform to the external reality to which it relates. This great truth is revealed in the statements, "Let the weak say, I am strong" (Joel 3:10).

Look back over the good resolutions with which many past new years are encumbered. They lived a little while and then they died. Why? Because they were severed from their root. Assume that you are that which you want to be. Experience in imagination what you would experience in the flesh were you already that which you want to be. Remain faithful to your assumption, so that you define yourself as that which you have assumed. Things have no life if they are severed from their roots, and our consciousness, our "I AM-ness" is the root of all that springs in our world.

"If we believe not that I am he, ye shall die in your sins" (John 8:24), that is, if I do not believe that I am already that which I desire to be, then I remain as I am and die in my present concept of self. There is no power, outside of the consciousness of man, to resurrect and make alive that which man desires to experience. That man who is accustomed to call up at will whatever images he pleases, will be, by virtue of the power of his imagination, master of his fate.

> I am the resurrection, and the life; he that believeth in Me, though he were dead, yet shall he live.
>
> —JOHN 11:25

> Ye shall know the truth, and the truth shall make you free.   —JOHN 8:32

4.

No One to Change
But Self

And for their sakes I sanctify myself, that they also
might be sanctified through the truth.

—John 17:19

THE ideal we serve and strive to attain could never
be evolved from us were it not potentially involved
in our nature.

It is now my purpose to retell and to emphasize an
experience of mine that occurred several years ago. I
believe that *The Search* (originally published as a sepa-
rate pamphlet) will help us to understand the opera-
tion of the law of consciousness, and show us that we
have no one to change but self.

THE SEARCH

ONCE in an idle interval at sea, I meditated on "the perfect state," and wondered what I would be, were I of too pure eyes to behold iniquity, if to me all things were pure and were I without condemnation. As I became lost in this fiery brooding, I found myself lifted above the dark environment of the senses. So intense was the feeling, I felt myself a being of fire dwelling in a body of air. Voices as from a heavenly chorus, with the exaltation of those who had been conquerors in a conflict with death, were singing "He is risen, He is risen," and intuitively I knew they meant me.

Then I seemed to be walking in the night. I soon came upon a scene that might have been the ancient Pool of Bethesda, for in this place lay a great multitude of impotent folk—blind, halt, withered—waiting not for the moving of the water as of tradition, but waiting for me. As I came near, without thought or effort on my part they were, one after the other, molded as by the Magician of the Beautiful. Eyes, hands, feet—all missing members—were drawn from some invisible reservoir and molded in harmony with that perfection which I felt springing within me. When all were made perfect, the chorus exulted, "It is finished." Then the scene dissolved and I awoke.

I know this vision was the result of my intense meditation upon the idea of perfection, for my meditations invariably bring about union with the state contemplated. I had been so completely absorbed within the idea that for a while I had become what I contemplated, and the high purpose with which I had for that moment identified myself drew the companionship of high things and fashioned the vision in harmony with my inner nature. The ideal with which we are united works by association of ideas to awaken a thousand moods to create a drama in keeping with the central idea.

I first discovered this close relationship of moods to vision when I was aged about seven. I became aware of a mysterious life quickening within me like a stormy ocean of frightening might. I always knew when I would be united with this hidden identity, for my senses were expectant on the nights of these visitations and I knew beyond all doubt that before morning I would be alone with immensity. I so dreaded these visitations that I would lie awake until my eyes from sheer exhaustion closed. As my eyes closed in sleep, I was no longer solitary but smitten through and through with another being, and yet I knew it to be myself. It seemed older than life, yet nearer to me than my boyhood. If I tell what I discovered on these nights, I do so not to impose my ideas on others but that I may give hope to those who seek the law of life.

I discovered that my expectant mood worked as a magnet to unite me with this Greater Me, while my fears made It appear as a stormy sea. As a boy, I conceived of this mysterious self as might, and in my union with It I felt its majesty as a stormy sea which drenched me, then rolled and tossed me as a helpless wave.

As a man I conceived of It as love and myself the son of It, and in my union with It, now, what a love enfolds me! It is a mirror to all. Whatever we conceive It as being, that It is to us. I believe It to be the center through which all the threads of the universe are drawn; therefore I have altered my values and changed my ideas so that they now depend upon and are in harmony with this sole cause of all that is. It is to me that changeless reality which fashions circumstances in harmony with our concepts of ourselves.

My mystical experiences have convinced me that there is no way to bring about the outer perfection we seek other than by the transformation of ourselves.

As soon as we succeed in transforming ourselves, the world will melt magically before our eyes and reshape itself in harmony with that which our transformation affirms.

Two other visions I will tell because they bear out the truth of my assertion that we, by intensity of love and hate, become what we contemplate.

Once, with closed eyes made radiant from brooding, I meditated on the eternal question, "Who Am I?" and felt myself gradually dissolve into a shoreless sea of vibrant light, imagination passing beyond all fear of death. In this state nothing existed but myself, a boundless ocean of liquid light. Never have I felt more intimate with Being. How long this experience lasted I do not know, but my return to earth was accompanied by a distinct feeling of crystallizing again into human shape.

At another time, I lay on my bed and with my eyes shut as in sleep I brooded on the mystery of Buddha. In a little while, the dark caverns of my brain began to grow luminous. I seemed to be surrounded by luminous clouds which emanated from my head as fiery, pulsating rings. I saw nothing but these luminous rings for a time. Then there appeared before my eyes a rock of quartz crystal. While I gazed upon it, the crystal broke into pieces which invisible hands quickly shaped into the living Buddha. As I looked on this meditative figure, I saw that it was myself. I was the living Buddha whom I contemplated. A light like the sun glowed from this living image of myself with increasing intensity until it exploded. Then the light gradually faded and once more I was back within the blackness of my room.

Out of what sphere or treasury of design came this being mightier than human, his garments, the crystal, the light? If I saw, heard and moved in a world of real beings when I seemed to myself to be walking in the night, when the lame, the halt, the blind were transformed in harmony with my inner nature, then I am justified in assuming that I have a more subtile body than the physical, a body that can be detached from the physical and used in other spheres; for to see, to hear, to move are functions of an organism however ethereal. If I brood over the alternative that my psychic experiences were self-begotten fantasy, no less am I moved to wonder at this mightier self who flashes on my mind a drama as real as those I experience when I am fully awake.

On these fiery meditations I have entered again and again, and I know beyond all doubt that both assumptions are true. Housed within this form of earth is a body attuned to a world of light, and I have, by intense meditation, lifted it as with a magnet through the skull of this dark house of flesh. The first time I awoke the fires within me I thought my head would explode. There was intense vibration at the base of my skull, then sudden oblivion of all. Then I found myself clothed in a garment of light and attached by a silvery elastic cord to the slumbering body on the bed. So exalted were my feelings, I felt related to the stars. In this garment I roamed spheres more familiar than earth, but found that, as on earth, conditions were molded in harmony with my nature. "Self-begotten fantasy," I hear you say. No more so than the things of earth. I am an immortal being conceiving myself as man and forming worlds in the likeness and image of my concept of self.

What we imagine, that we are. By our imagination, we have created this dream of life, and by our imagination we will re-enter that eternal world of light, becoming that which we were before we imagined the world. In the divine economy nothing is lost. We cannot lose anything save by descent from the sphere where the thing has its natural life. There is no transforming power in death and, whether we are here or there, we fashion the world that surrounds us by the intensity of our imagination and feeling, and we illuminate or darken our lives by the concepts we hold of ourselves. Nothing is more important to us than our conception of ourselves, and especially is this true of our concept of the deep, hidden One within us.

Those that help or hinder us, whether they know it or not, are the servants of that law which shapes outward circumstances in harmony with our inner nature. It is our conception of ourselves which frees or constrains us, though it may use material agencies to achieve its purpose.

Because life molds the outer world to reflect the inner arrangement of our minds, there is no way of bringing about the outer perfection we seek other than by the transformation of ourselves. No help cometh from without; the hills to which we lift our eyes are those of an inner range. It is thus to our own consciousness that we must turn as to the only reality, the only foundation on which all phenomena can be explained. We can rely absolutely on the justice of this law to give us only that which is of the nature of ourselves

To attempt to change the world before we change our concept of ourselves is to struggle against the nature of things. There can be no outer change until there is first an inner change. As within, so without. I am not advocating philosophical indifference when I suggest that we should imagine ourselves as already that which we want to be, living in a mental atmosphere of greatness, rather than using physical means and arguments to bring about the desired change. Everything we do, unaccompanied by a change of consciousness, is but futile readjustment of surfaces. However we toil or struggle, we can receive no more than our subconscious assumptions affirm. To protest against anything which happens to us is to protest against the law of our being and our rulership over our own destiny.

The circumstances of my life are too closely related to my conception of myself not to have been launched by my own spirit from some magical storehouse of my being. If there is pain to me in these happenings, I should look within myself for the cause, for I am moved here and there and made to live in a world in harmony with my concept of myself.

Intense meditation brings about a union with the state contemplated, and during this union we see visions, have experiences, and behave in keeping with our change of consciousness. This shows us that a transformation of consciousness will result in a change of environment and behavior. However, our ordinary alterations of consciousness, as we pass from one state to another, are not transformations, because each of them is so rapidly succeeded by another in the reverse direction; but whenever one state grows so stable as to definitely expel its rivals, then that central habitual state defines the character and is a true transformation. To say that we are transformed means that ideas previously peripheral in our consciousness now take a central place and form the habitual center of our energy.

All wars prove that violent emotions are extremely potent in precipitating mental rearrangements. Every great conflict has been followed by an era of materialism and greed in which the ideals for which the conflict ostensibly was waged are submerged. This is inevitable because war evokes hate, which impels a descent in consciousness from the plane of the ideal to the level where the conflict is waged. If we would become as emotionally aroused over our ideals as we become over our dislikes, we would ascend to the plane of our ideals as easily as we now descend to the level of our hates.

Love and hate have a magical transforming power, and we grow through their exercise into the likeness of what we contemplate. By intensity of hatred we create in ourselves the character we imagine in our enemies.

Qualities die for want of attention, so the unlovely states might best be rubbed out by imagining "beauty for ashes and joy for mourning" (Isaiah 61:3) rather than by direct attacks on the state from which we would be free. "Whatsoever things are lovely and of good report, think on these things" (Philippians 4:8), for we become that with which we are *en rapport*.

There is nothing to change but our concept of self. Humanity is a single being in spite of its many forms and faces, and there is in it only such seeming separation as we find in our own being when we are dreaming. The pictures and circumstances we see in dreams are creations of our own imagination and have no existence save in ourselves. The same is true of the pictures and circumstances we see in this dream of life. They reveal our concepts of ourselves. As soon as we succeed in transforming self, our world will dissolve and reshape itself in harmony with that which our change affirms.

The universe which we study with such care is a dream, and we the dreamers of the dream, eternal dreamers dreaming non-eternal dreams. One day, like Nebuchadnezzar, we shall awaken from the dream, from the nightmare in which we fought with demons, to find that we really never left our eternal home; that we were never born and have never died save in our dream.

Made in United States
Cleveland, OH
21 June 2025

17853643R20030